C000071686

FAITH AND MENTAL HEALTH

FR BILLY SWAN

*All booklets are published
thanks to the generosity of the supporters
of the Catholic Truth Society*

CATHOLIC TRUTH SOCIETY

PUBLISHERS TO THE HOLY SEE

FAITH AND
MENTAL HEALTH

All rights reserved. First published 2020 by The Incorporated Catholic Truth Society, 40-46 Harleyford Road London SE11 5AY Tel: 020 7640 0042 Fax: 020 7640 0046. Website: www.ctsbooks.org. Copyright © 2020 The Incorporated Catholic Truth Society.

ISBN 978 1 78469 640 5

Contents

Introduction

The importance of our mental health has been highlighted widely in recent years. This is a welcome and necessary development. Professional voices from psychology, psychiatry and medicine have all argued for increasing awareness of the importance of mental health and the need for greater support structures to help people with mental health problems. I believe that the Church is one body that has still to find her voice on this crucial topic. This is lamentable for the wisdom of the Gospel and faith Tradition of the Church have much light to shed on the issue of mental health.

This booklet aims to help the Church make a strong contribution to this area of human wellbeing and to do so with confidence. Such confidence is born from a conviction that what she offers is of great value. This publication seeks to engage the reader by offering ten ways in which Christian faith contributes to a sound mental health. These ten ways are not exhaustive but the beginning of a conversation and pointers to a life-giving resource that contributes significantly to a balanced and wholesome life. Before we begin our journey to explore these benefits, it is first necessary to preface our argument with three important caveats. The first of these caveats points out the obvious, namely that having faith does not immunise us from mental health problems. The proof of this is found with heroic people of faith who suffered from mental health issues. Here I briefly mention three.[1]

The first is St Louis Martin (1823-1894), the father of St Thérèse of Lisieux. In her autobiography *The Story of a Soul*, St Thérèse wrote affectionately about her father but at one point referred to him drinking "the most bitter and humiliating of all chalices". This suffering of her father was his committal to a mental institution on the 12th February 1889.[2] Despite this trial, the holiness and faith of Louis Martin was affirmed by Thérèse herself and documented in sixteen letters that he wrote. These were in addition to many more from his wife Zélie that give details about his life of faith and prayer.[3]

---

[1] I am indebted to Aaron Kheriaty's book *The Catholic Guide to Depression* (Sophia Press, New Hampshire, 2012) for clarifying these caveats. This book is a pioneering work of looking at depression and mental illness through the lens of the Catholic faith.

[2] See J. Clarke, ed., *The Story of a Soul: The Autobiography of St Thérèse of Lisieux*, ICS Publications, Washington DC, 1972, p. 156.

[3] In 2011, the letters of Zélie and Louis Martin were published in English as *A Call to a Deeper Love: The Family Correspondence of the Parents of Saint Thérèse of the Child Jesus, 1863–1885*, Alba House, London, 2011. On the 8th October 2015, Louis Martin was canonised a saint of the Church together with his wife Zélie, becoming the first spouses in the Church's history to be canonized.

St Benedict Joseph Labré (1783-1818) was born in north-eastern France towards the end of the eighteenth century. He tried persistently to become a monk and enter religious life but was refused each time. It is thought that the manifestation of certain psychological or even psychiatric symptoms was the reason why he was deemed unsuitable for the way of life to which he aspired. Despite this, he went to Rome where he spent the last six years of his life on the streets among the poor and homeless. When he died in 1818 aged 35, crowds gathered in the streets and chanted, "*È morto il santo*...the saint is dead".[4]

Gerard Manley Hopkins SJ was born in 1844 and died in 1889. This English poet and Jesuit priest is widely regarded as one of finest poets of his age, whose many works of beauty were at times composed while experiencing long bouts of depression. Many of his sonnets outline his struggle with religious doubt and feelings of estrangement from God. Nevertheless, his works also display a faith that transcended his darkness into hope.[5]

---

[4] Cited in B. Groeschel, *The Saints in My Life*, Our Sunday Visitor, Indiana, 2011, p. 131.

[5] For a summary of Hopkins' faith minted in darkness, see C. Randall, *A Heart Lost in Wonder: The Life and Faith of Gerard Manley Hopkins*, SPCK, London, 2020.

What the lives of Louis Martin, Benedict Labré and Gerard Manley Hopkins demonstrate is that people of faith are not spared from mental health difficulties. While this might initially sound disappointing, what it invites us to consider is how faith helps us deal with mental health challenges – not by-passing them or avoiding them but facing them courageously and navigating our way through them with God's grace. This way, people of faith are in a better position to dialogue compassionately with our brothers and sisters who also suffer in their minds but who have less faith, a different faith or none at all.

The second caveat is that not every mental illness has a spiritual cause, so having weak faith or no faith is not necessarily the cause of poor mental health. It is important to clarify this because although we can demonstrate how faith can benefit mental health, we cannot show that a lack of faith is the cause of problems in this area. This caveat ought to pepper our argument with humility and rid it of any triumphalist tone as if faith were a ready-made set of answers to complex questions.

The final caveat insists that religious or spiritual therapy is never a substitute for medical treatment for mental illnesses. Mental health is best served by a holistic care of the person's body, mind and spirit. That said, while spiritual therapy is never a substitute for medical intervention, neither can medical intervention, on its own, be sufficient. Any materialistic reduction of the human person is not consistent with how we understand who God created us to be. The teachings of Vatican II and the *Catechism of the Catholic Church* are clear:

> "Man is made of body and soul...the unity of soul and body is so profound that one has to consider the soul to be the form of the body: i.e., it is because of the spiritual soul that that the body made of matter becomes a living human body; spirit and matter, in man, are not two natures united, but rather their union forms a single nature".[6]

This understanding of the human person is key to how we approach the treatment of mental health and indeed our wellbeing in general – physical, mental and spiritual. Having a clear understanding of the human person directs and governs the course of treatment when things go wrong. For this reason, the Church advocates the holistic care of the person as a unity of body and soul with the care of both elements recognised as being important. We are more than flesh and blood. Not all our problems can be cured by medicine and pills.

---

[6] *Gaudium et spes*, 14; *Catechism of the Catholic Church*, 365. Hereafter abbreviated to *CCC*.

And so with these caveats in mind, the following ten chapters try to show how faith can be an invaluable resource for improving and sustaining our mental health. According to a 1992 review article in the *American Journal of Psychiatry*, 72% of studies found a positive association between religious commitment and mental health.[7] Let us explore why this might be the case.

---

[7] D.B. Larson-K.A. Sherrill-J.S. Lyons-F.C. Craigie-S.B. Thielman-M.A. Greenwold-S.S. Larson, eds., 'Associations between dimensions of religious commitment and mental health reported in the American Journal of Psychiatry and Archives of General Psychiatry: 1978-1989' in *American Journal of Psychiatry*, 149 (1992), pp. 557-559.

1. The Offer and Acceptance of God's Unconditional Love

The first and most basic message of the Christian faith is the pronouncement that we are accepted and loved unconditionally by God. In the Bible, St John reminds us of two of the most foundational doctrines of the whole Christian Gospel. First, that "God is Love" (*1 Jn* 4:8) - not that God is like love or does love but rather He is love itself. God's essence and nature is love at the core. The second follows on from this, that "God loved us first" (*1 Jn* 4:19). God's love precedes anything we can ever say or do by way of response. Christians believe that God loving us does not depend on us earning that love by how we behave. This is the love of God revealed in Jesus Christ and the gift that is continually offered to all in every place and time.

This message has become so familiar to us that its power to change us no longer has the effect it should. It has become so domesticated that we fail to grasp its full potential. Yet it remains a revolutionary message that changes lives every day. To the youth of the

Church, Pope Francis spoke these words: "The very first truth I would tell each of you is this: 'God loves you'. It makes no difference whether you have already heard it or not. I want to remind you of it. God loves you. Never doubt this, whatever may happen to you in life. At every moment, you are infinitely loved".[8]

This declaration that we are loved by another is a positive, hopeful and transformative truth that addresses our human existence at every level. To be loved and love in return is essential for our emotional lives, for our emotions draw us into loving relationships which give us life and joy. Believing we are loved implies that no matter how we are feeling, how well or sick we become, God's love is ever available and accessible in a deeply personal and consistent way. Here is an inexhaustible source of self-esteem and positive energy that cannot be replicated by our own efforts. It is sheer gift.

The assurance of God's unconditional love is given because of who he has declared us to be – beloved children of God our Father who possess the goodness and beauty of God himself. As we are His children, His Spirit of love has been poured into our hearts making us cry out "Abba Father!" (*Rm* 5:5; *Ga* 4:6) Yes, we are broken, limited and in need of healing and mercy, yet our faith tells us that, no matter how chaotic our lives

---

8 Pope Francis, *Christ is Alive*, 112.

seem or what our past has been, the love of Christ never stops pursuing us, offering itself to us again and again. God's love for us is not static but searching and dynamic; it is the love of the good shepherd who goes in search of the lost sheep (cf. *Lk* 15:4ff) or the woman in search of the lost coin (*Lk* 15:8-10). In the beautiful words of St Augustine (354-430),

> "You have called to me, and have cried out and have shattered my deafness...You have sent forth fragrance, I have drawn in my breath and I pant after you. I have tasted you and I hunger and thirst after you. You have touched me and I have burned for your peace".[9]

Therefore, as we endure any difficulty, mental or physical, our faith assures us that "nothing can separate us from the love of God, made visible in Christ Jesus our Lord" (*Rm* 8:39).

The second half of this foundational theme of God's unconditional love is whether and how it is accepted by us as gift. The experience of love consists in its being offered *and* received. I might be told of God's love towards me but do I really believe it and accept it? We all know that faith in God's goodness is severely tested at times of trial and crisis. In periods of great

---

[9] *Confessions*, 10, 27, 38 in J.K. Ryan, ed. and trans., *The Confessions of Saint Augustine*, Image Books, New York, 1960, pp. 254-255.

suffering we might be tempted to ask, "If God loves me then where is He now?" Or we might resort to the language of merit – on one hand to ask ourselves, "What have I done to deserve this?" or on the other hand to say, "I deserve this because I'm a bad person". What makes a gracious acceptance of God's love easier is to realise that God's love for us does not depend on how good we are. He loves us not because we are good but so that we might be good as He is good.

His love is also constant whether we are happy or sad. He does not love us less in the darkness. When we suffer we are not being punished for our past or victimised for what we haven't done. We know this from the life of Jesus himself and his own suffering though he was innocent of sin. As disciples who participate in his Passion, Jesus leads us on his path and invites us to follow him. On this path and united to his Spirit, we partake in his suffering and the new life he won for us. What we suffer is a participation in the great mystery of his cross that leads to a share in his resurrection. It is a mystery that is greater than any of us for it is part of the transformation not just of us but of the whole world. That is why St Paul understood his trials beyond himself as a completion of "what is lacking in Christ's afflictions for the sake of his body, that is, the Church" (*Col* 1:24). Therefore, for the one suffering from physical or mental illness, the experience of darkness is an invitation to know the Lord Jesus by "sharing in his sufferings" (*Ph* 3:11) and with him to offer our pain for the love for all humanity. Here is the mystery of love that is inseparably woven with suffering but that leads to hope and the promise of new life.

Finally, a word on the power of faith as trust in divine providence and the freedom from anxiety that comes with that. We human beings are free and responsible. Yet we know from experience that while we can plan and decide as wisely as we can, there are still many variables that are outside our control. We fail, get sick and unexpected things happen. For the person of no faith, the urge to control everything brings with it a great deal of stress and anxiety. If there is no God or no divine providence then all the pressure falls back on us. This added pressure impacts negatively on our mental health.

Faith in God's providence and goodness does not absolve us of our responsibilities but assures us that the future is bigger than any of us. Through all the events of life, the person of faith in God receives Jesus' words with great hope for they know that they do not face their challenges alone: "Do not let your hearts be troubled. Trust in God still and trust in me" (*Jn* 14:1); "Come to me all you who labour and are overburdened and I will give you rest. Shoulder my yoke and learn from me, for I am gentle and humble of heart and you will find rest in your souls. Yes, my yoke is easy and my burden light" (*Mt* 11:28-30). The person of faith can also make these words of St Paul their own: "We know that by turning everything to their good God co-operates with all those who love him" (*Rm* 8:28). Here is a confidence consistent with the words of Jesus himself who explicitly urges us not to burden our minds with things beyond our control but to trust in Him and focus instead on being at rights with God and the coming of his kingdom:

> "That is why I am telling you not to worry about your life and what you are to eat, nor your body and how you are to cloth it...Can any of you, for all his worrying, add one single cubit to his span of life?...Set you hearts on his kingdom first, and his righteousness, and all these other things will be given you as well. So do not worry about tomorrow; tomorrow will take care of itself. Each day has enough trouble of its own" (*Mt* 6:25-34).

This is why the second and third steps of the "Twelve Step Programme" of Alcoholics Anonymous are invitations to co-operate with and entrust oneself to our "Higher Power". Here is one of the best examples of coming to realise that we can't do it all on our own.

In conclusion, this chapter began with the foundational message of the Gospel as revealed by Jesus – the offer of God's unconditional love that has the power to change lives. May the continual offer of God's unconditional love be accepted by us with gratitude and joy. And may we surrender ourselves with confidence and peace to his goodness which triumphs in the end.

2. Christ Reveals us to Ourselves

The second and related resource of our faith is that it declares us to be someone, helping us understand ourselves in relation to another. The human person is a mystery to be revered. We never quite arrive at the point of fully knowing ourselves, let alone knowing others. There is always something more to discover and become aware of. The challenge of knowing ourselves is also complicated by our needs and desires that can obscure an accurate understanding of who we are. Honesty forces us to admit that we humans have the tendency to see what we want to see and not what is there to see.

The life and teachings of Jesus of Nazareth reveal that we are more than our strengths and weaknesses, lights and shadows. My being as a child of God "should be the truth through which I see clearly everything else about my life, my circumstances, my emotional state, my vocation and my destiny, even my depression".[10]

---

[10] A. Kheriaty, *The Catholic Guide to Depression*, p. 205.

This truth implies that if we are children of another and not our own creation, then we must look to the One who created us to understand who we are. Only the word of another outside us can hold up a mirror and help us see a truth that we can't see ourselves. For Christians, this external mirror is none other than the Word made flesh, Jesus Christ (cf. *Jn* 1:14). By his life, death and resurrection, Jesus not only revealed God to us but he also revealed us to ourselves. With his encounters with people, his teaching, parables, suffering and death, Jesus masterfully revealed sides of our human condition in dramatic and unexpected ways. In the Jewish religious tradition of his time, the external observance of the law took on an exaggerated importance at the expense of the disposition of the heart and the motive of love. Jesus' teaching was radical for he proposed that being at rights with God involves making the inner journey of awareness of what truly motivates us and requires cleansing the heart of evil intentions and self-interests (cf. *Mt* 15:11; *Mk* 7:15). For those who wished Jesus to be a political Messiah, this interior battleground was not what they expected. Yet from the accounts of his Passion, we see that the cacophony of sin, injustice, betrayal and human dysfunction on terrible display can only be healed by his saving grace that penetrates into the heart of that fallen nature in which we all share.

In order to begin that process of healing with God, Jesus asks us to be humble and to know our need for him. He taught us that pride blinds us while humility helps us to see. To the Pharisees who thought they understood and who boasted, "We are not blind surely?" Jesus said, "Blind? If you were, you would not be guilty but since you say 'we see' your guilt remains" (*Jn* 9:41). On the other end of the spectrum, Jesus saw the good and the potential in people like Zacchaeus and the woman caught in adultery, whom people had written off and condemned – "This too is a child of Abraham" (*Lk* 19:10); "Neither do I condemn you" (*Jn* 8:11).

To help us come to terms with our pride, many of the greatest saints of the Church made this painful journey before us. In his *Soliloquies*, St Augustine summed up the entire spiritual life in this prayer: "O God, always the same, let me know myself, let me know you. This is prayer".[11] And when Augustine received the grace he prayed for to know himself, not all he saw was pretty. He wrote, "Lord, you turned my attention back to myself…and I looked and was appalled…You thrust me before my own eyes so that I

---

[11] *Soliloquies*, 2, 1, 1. Cited in D.X. Burt, ed., *Let Me Know Myself: Reflections on the Prayer of Augustine*, Liturgical Press, Minnesota, 2002, p. viii.

should discover my iniquity and hate it".[12] Augustine's honest confrontation with himself in God's light was not an end in itself but a prelude to the transformation of a man who came to know God as beauty, mercy and peace. According to St Bonaventure (1221-1274), "I know myself better in God than in myself".[13] St Bernard of Clairvaux (1090-1153) summed up our need to know ourselves before God when he humbly acknowledged, "I need truth that I may not be able to hide from Him, and the grace that I may not wish to hide from Him".[14] Here Bernard named something that the rest of us are slow to admit – that we need God's truth to reveal to us what is real and his grace to save us from self-deception. For St Catherine of Siena (1347-1380), we cannot be our own interpreters for "we can see neither our own dignity nor the defects which spoil the beauty of our soul, unless we look at ourselves in the peaceful sea of God's being in which

---

[12] *Confessions*, 8, 7, 16 in J.K. Ryan, ed. and trans., *The Confessions of Saint Augustine*, p. 193.

[13] *Hexaemeron*, 12, 9. Cited in I. Delio, *Simply Bonaventure: An Introduction to his Life, Thought and Writings*, New City Press, New York, 2001, p. 72.

[14] *On the Song of Songs*, 74, 8. Cited in P. Murray, *In the Grip of Light*, Bloomsbury, London, 2012, p. 73.

we are imaged".[15] Catherine also spoke about "the gentle mirror of God" in which we catch a glimpse of the true dignity of our nature.[16]

Centuries later, the Second Vatican Council stated that "it is only in the mystery of the Word made flesh that the mystery of humanity truly becomes clear".[17] In a direct challenge to modern attempts to define ourselves in isolation from the Creator, Pope Benedict XVI taught that "without God, man neither knows which way to go, nor even understands who he is".[18]

The critical point to be made here from the Scriptures and the faith Tradition of the Church is the impossibility of knowing ourselves apart from God and the truth revealed in the Gospel. We need a mirror and doctor to do this – a mirror to help us to see all that is true and a doctor of the body and soul who prescribes how we need to recover and to stay healthy with his grace. For the Christian, we rejoice in the gift of Christ who is that mirror and is that doctor who tenderly leads us to know ourselves and shows us the way to improve, grow and flourish.

[15] 'Look at Yourself in the Water' in M. O'Driscoll, ed., *Catherine of Siena: Passion for the Truth: Compassion for Humanity. Selected Spiritual Writings*, New City Press, New York, 2005, p. 36.
[16] *Dialogue*, 13 in M. O'Driscoll, ed., *Catherine of Siena: Passion for the Truth*, p. 99.
[17] *Gaudium et spes*, 22.
[18] *Caritas in veritate*, 78.

But how do we grow and flourish? The great spiritual Tradition of the Church offers us three pathways in our quest to grow towards this maturity and holiness. St Paul described this process as growing in "[Christ's] likeness from one degree of glory to another" (2 *Co* 3:18). For the Christian, this involves a process of transformation that takes place along the paths of purgation (being freed from harmful attachments that obstruct our growth); illumination (seeing all there is to see and understanding all there is to be understood) and perfect union with God as love.[19] A crucially important and relevant point to our topic is that in order to negotiate these stages of growth, some degree of emotional and mental pain is inevitable. It is part of growing up, maturing and becoming more perfect in love.

This understanding of ourselves poses a challenge to our postmodern culture that places a strong emphasis on the self. We hear about helping yourself, being yourself and asserting yourself. There is also an increasing focus on self-invention – becoming ʰo you want to be by the power of the will. While ʰ of this is good, over-emphasis risks acting from ˡ desires that can change and telling ourselves ˠt to hear, even when it is disconnected

ᵉ the subject of a book by Ralph Martin, *The* ᵐaus Road, Ohio, 2006.

from reality. In contrast, faith in Christ reveals who we are and shows us how to be authentically human in accordance with our nature made in God's image and likeness. This frees us from anxiety and the impossible task of trying to understand ourselves only in relation to ourselves.

The Gospel is good news for it frees us from the confusion of not knowing who we are, where we have come from or where we are going. For the person of faith, everything unfolds along the journey of life that we walk as fellow pilgrims, empowered with the fundamental truth of our identity as God's beloved children, brothers and sisters in Christ and destined to share eternal life with him.

3. Faith as Source of Meaning

There is broad agreement that there exists in humanity a universal need for meaning.[20] There is also broad evidence that a lack of meaning in human lives tends to undermine our mental health. According to psychiatrist Andrew Sims, "Lack or loss of meaning in life is probably the most frequent spiritual symptom voiced by our patients".[21] This point was powerfully argued by Victor Frankl in his book *Man's Search for Meaning* where he observed that those who had the best chance of surviving the horrors of Auschwitz were those who could find meaning in their suffering. With Nietzsche, Frankl argued that "the person who has a 'why' to live for can bear with almost any how".[22] In his book, Frankl poignantly shared with his readers

---

[20] See M.F. Steger, 'Meaning in Life' in S.J. Lopez, ed., *Oxford Handbook of Positive Psychology*, Oxford University Press, Oxford, 2009, pp. 679-687.

[21] A. Sims, *Is Faith Delusion? Why Religion is Good for your Health*, Continuum, London, 2009, p. 46.

[22] V. Frankl, *Man's Search for Meaning*, Rider Books, London, 2004, p. 109.

that the love of his wife was what gave meaning to his suffering and gave him the strength to live.[23] Having survived the war, Frankl went on to develop a therapy known as 'Logotherapy' based on helping people find meaning in their lives and reasons to live.

Not everyone would agree that such meaning exists. For many contemporary atheists, there is no God and therefore no meaning. For Jean-Paul Sartre (1905-1980), "Here we sit, all of us, eating and drinking to preserve our precious existence and really there is nothing, nothing, absolutely no reason for existing".[24] Similarly for the English scientist Richard Dawkins, "the universe has no design, no purpose, no evil and no good, nothing but blind, pitiless indifference".[25] But if life has no meaning then there are no answers to the ultimate questions of identity – who am I?; of value – do I matter?; of purpose – why am I here? and agency – can I make a difference? This would seem to condemn us to a life of frustration by seeking truths that can never be found. As Andrew Sims testifies from his experience as a psychiatrist, "Profound suffering in

---

[23] "Nothing could touch the strength of my love, my thoughts, and the image of my beloved". *Man's Search for Meaning*, p. 50.

[24] J.P. Sartre, *Nausea*, New Directions Publishing, New York, 1964, p.112.

[25] R. Dawkins, *River out of Eden: A Darwinian view of life*, Basic Books, New York, 1995, p. 133.

the lives of many with mental illness is caused by a feeling of meaninglessness".[26]

The Gospel insists that life has meaning and that every human life is meaningful. In the words of St John Henry Newman (1801-1890), "God has created me to do him some definitive service; he has committed some work to me which he has not committed to another. I have my mission".[27] This concern about the loss of meaning in Western culture was taken up by St John Paul II (1920-2005) when he described depression as a "disease often accompanied by an existential and spiritual crisis that leads to an inability to perceive the meaning of life".[28] In more recent times, Pope Francis reminded the whole Church that our lives do have meaning because "I am a mission on this earth; that is the reason I am here in this world".[29] If everyone's life is a mission then this mission originates in the love of God of me and his purposes for me. Pope Francis explains, "Discernment has to do with the meaning of

---

[26] A. Sims, *Is Faith a Delusion?*, p. 215.

[27] St John Henry Newman, 'The Mission of My Life' in T. de Bertodano, ed., *Treasury of the Catholic Church*, Darton, Longmann & Todd, London, 1999, p. 190.

[28] Pope John Paul II, *Address to the Participants in the 18th International Conference Promoted by the Pontifical Council for Health and Pastoral Care on the Theme of Depression*, 14th November 2003.

[29] Pope Francis, *The Joy of the Gospel*, 273. See also *Christ is Alive*, 254.

my life before the Father who knows and loves me, and with the real purpose of my life, which nobody knows better than he".[30] These voices combine powerfully to argue that belief in a personal God of love opens our eyes to the inherent meaning in every human life. "We are not some casual and meaningless product of evolution. Each of us is the result of a thought of God. Each of us is willed, each of us is loved, each of us is necessary".[31]

In John's Gospel, Jesus is described as "the light who has come into the world…the true light that enlightens all people" (1:9). Later in the same Gospel Jesus describes himself as "the light of the world. Whoever follows me will not walk in darkness but will have the light of life" (8:12). Continuing with the image of light, the following is St Paul's prayer for Christians – that Christ may "enlighten the eyes of your mind so you can see what hope his call holds for you" (*Ep* 1:18). This Christian enlightenment is not a superior form of knowledge or an elite possession of truth. Rather it is the grace to discern meaning in the world and in the events of life. It is to recognise a common thread in all created reality which affirms its intelligibility and coherence. C.S. Lewis (1898-1963)

---

[30] Pope Francis, *Rejoice and Be Glad*, 170.

[31] Pope Benedict XVI, *Homily at Mass for the Beginning of the Petrine Ministry*, 24th April 2005.

puts it this way: "I believe in Christianity as I believe that the sun has risen, not only because I see it but because by it, I see everything else".[32]

For Lewis, a favourite way he uncovered this inherent meaning in human experience was through story and narratives that he masterfully employed in writings such as *The Chronicles of Narnia*. But he and others would point out that the greatest story of them all was to be found in Scripture where the revelation of God in Christ and our relationship to him is the key to discovering the meaning of our existence. The importance of understanding the narrative of Scripture is complemented by our participation within that narrative – a participation that opens up to a vision of who we are that is higher and more noble than we could ever imagine.

The quest to discover meaning in our lives is one that we all have to undertake. However, for the Christian, we do so in continuity with some of the greatest minds, thinkers and saints in the history of the Church who grappled with the same ultimate questions of meaning before us. Engaging with their thought and perspectives on experiences like suffering, love and death means that we do not have to start from scratch but can "see with other eyes, imagine

---

[32] 'Is Theology Poetry?' in C.S. Lewis, *Essay Collection*, Collins, London, 2000, p. 21.

with other imaginations and feel with other hearts as well as our own".[33]

The glad tidings of Christian faith are that it confirms our deepest instincts that facts, information and data just aren't enough. We hunger for meaning. In a world that craves new experiences, we can identify more with T.S. Eliot's lament: "We had the experience but missed the meaning".[34] Our faith in Christ helps us understand our story but also helps us see that we participate in the great story of salvation that continues to unfold. For this reason "Christianity does not simply make sense to us; it also makes sense of us. It positions us in the great narrative of cosmic history and locates us on a map of meaning".[35]

[33] C.S. Lewis, *An Experiment in Criticism*, Cambridge University Press, Cambridge, 1992, p. 137.

[34] T.S. Eliot, *The Dry Salvages*, Faber & Faber, London, 1941.

[35] A. McGrath, *Surprised by Meaning*, John Knox Press, Kentucky, 2011, p. 114.

4. 'He Became Human so that We Might Become God'

Afundamental belief of Christianity is that every human experience has been touched and transformed by the God who became human. This includes depression and mental illness. Christian faith in the incarnation says that in Jesus Christ, the two orders of humanity and divinity come together. By becoming human, God absorbed everything human into his own divine life. In the words of St Athanasius (296-373), "The Son of God became man so that we might become God".[36]

I remember during my first visit to the holy land, one of the highlights was a visit to the garden of Gethsemane and the Church of All Nations next to it. There in the chapel, we knelt at the large rock before the altar for an hour in prayer. Here was the rock on which Jesus, after the Last Supper on the night before

---

[36] Athanasius, *On the Incarnation*, 54, 3. Cited in M. J. Christensen-J.A. Wittung, eds., *Partakers of the Divine Nature,* Baker Academic, Michigan, 2007, p. 11.

he died, "fell on his face and prayed: 'Father if it is possible, let this cup pass me by. Nevertheless, let it be as you, not I, would have it'" (*Mt* 26:39-40). As I prayed there in that sacred place, the realisation dawned on me that this was the place where Jesus' Passion truly began. It struck me that before ever he received the first blow to his body, it was here that his agony began with the intense suffering of his mind. The Gospels tell us that at that time "a great sadness came over him and great distress. Then he said to them 'My soul is sorrowful to the point of death'" (*Mt* 26:37-38). Here as he entered his Passion, Jesus moved into the space of all who suffer in their minds. In this time, the Son of God joined all those who know the agony of worry, anxiety, fear and emotional pain. With Jesus' agony in the garden, God entered into the suffering of those who endure mental distress of any description in order to be with them and offer them hope.

Jesus' agony in the garden was not the first time he suffered emotionally or mentally. Earlier in the Gospels, the Lord was grieved when the disciples could not understand him (cf. *Mt* 17:17; *Mk* 9:19; *Lk* 9:41). He wept at the death of his friend Lazarus (*Jn* 11:35) and over Jerusalem, the city of David that would reject him (*Lk* 19:41). On Good Friday, at the height of his torment on the cross, he cried out: "My God, my God, why have you forsaken me?" (*Mt* 27:46; *Mk* 15:34). This cry of torment was not one of physical pain, excruciating as that certainly was. His agony was one of loneliness.

That Jesus entered into the space of those who suffer mentally is a sign of his great love and solidarity. It means that no matter how alone we feel or how isolated or misunderstood we are, he is with us in our darkness. He has been there before. What wounds us wounded him first. In the words of St John Paul II, "Christ took all human suffering on himself, even mental illness...This affliction configures the sick person to Christ and gives him/her a share in his redeeming Passion".[37] With the mental suffering of Jesus, God did not take away mental agony but filled it with his presence. Our God does not console us by abolishing anguish of the mind but by entering it and sharing it. United to us in our darkness, Jesus invites those of tortured mind to transcend the darkness with him towards the light of resurrection. For those who suffer in their minds, they have a friend and refuge in the sorrowful heart of Jesus in whose suffering they participate and in whose victory they will share.

In the Beatitudes, Jesus also teaches us the importance of tears: "Blessed are those who mourn

[37] Pope John Paul II, *Address to Participants at the International Conference Sponsored by the Pontifical Council for Pastoral Assistance to Health Care Workers*, 11th December 1996. Published in *L'Osservatore Romano*, (English edition), 11th December 1996.

for they shall be comforted" (*Mt* 5:5; *Lk* 6:21). With this beatitude Jesus teaches the paradox that in order to experience blessedness it is essential to mourn – to mourn what we lack, what we have lost and what we will never have. No one can have everything and there is a freedom in accepting that. Having much and trying to feel good all the time does not guarantee peace of mind. Feelings come and go but the blessedness Jesus speaks of is a more permanent state that leads to gratitude, harmony and joy. Tears may be painfully shed but they can help us accept the things we cannot change and to feel the pain of others. As Pope Francis writes beautifully, "Some realities in life are only seen with eyes cleansed with tears".[38]

Examples of two Christians might help here, one from the Catholic and another from the Orthodox tradition. For St John of the Cross (1542-1591), his *Dark Night of the Soul* describes the experience of interior pain caused by the loss of the experience of God, desolation, confusion, grief and anguish. Although distinct from clinical depression,[39] the image of darkness in the soul is one that those who suffer

---

[38] Pope Francis, *Christ is Alive*, 76.

[39] On the difference between the experience of the dark night and depression, see K. Culligan, 'The Dark Night and Depression' in K.J. Egan, ed., *Carmelite Prayer: A Tradition for the 21st Century*, Paulist Press, New York, 2003, pp. 119-139.

mentally will identify with. For John, this time of darkness and suffering is not an end in itself but offers the hope that what is in progress can be a purification of the senses, of one's image of God, of one's own attachments and one's ego. For John, this is caused by God's intimate presence who painfully but effectively makes us more perfect in love by transforming us to be more like Him: "O night that has united the Lover with his beloved, transforming the beloved in her Lover".[40]

In *The Gulag Archipelago*, the Russian novelist Aleksandr Solzhenitsyn (1918-2008) describes his imprisonment for criticising Soviet leader Josef Stalin. There he wrote not just about his sufferings but also about their meaning: "Bless you prison, bless you for being in my life. For there, lying upon the rotting straw, I came to realise that the object of life is not prosperity as we are made to believe, but the maturity of the human soul".[41]

For the person of faith, Jesus shows how suffering is not an end in itself but is a share in his own cross that serves the purpose of maturing us in preparation

---

[40] St John of the Cross, 'Dark Night of the Soul', 5 in K. Kavanagh-O. Rodriguez, eds., *The Collected Works of Saint John of the Cross*, ICS Publications, Washington DC, 1991, p. 359.

[41] Cited in D.M. Thomas, *Solzhenitsyn: A Century in his Life*, Little, Brown and Co., London, 1998, p. 194.

for a future that "God has prepared for those who love him" (*1 Co* 2:9). Christianity is good news for all who suffer from agony of the mind for it believes in a suffering servant who took on our "soul's anguish" (*Is* 53:11) and who transforms that anguish by love into hope. "By his wounds we have been healed" (*1 P* 2:24).

5. Forgiveness and Healing as Freedom

A fifth resource of faith is the transforming power of negative experiences such as sin, hurt and betrayal. Because of original sin, we human beings make mistakes, fail and love imperfectly. In our imperfection, at times we injure each other, leaving us wounded and in need of healing. Being wronged or hurt gives rise to strong emotions of anger and disappointment which, if not acknowledged and addressed, can lead to depression and other mental health problems. The famous psychologist Sigmund Freud (1856-1939) argued that much depression is caused by repressed anger. If this is true then all the more reason to address our anger and its root causes.

In the Gospels, forgiveness is a core teaching. Christians believe that Jesus Christ was sent into the world by the Father to forgive sins, heal relationships and "bring everything together under Christ as head" (*Ep* 1:10). Throughout his ministry, Jesus reveals a merciful God who desires to forgive sins and reconcile relationships that have been damaged. With his Spirit, the Lord also empowers us to forgive ourselves and each other as we have been forgiven by God (cf. *Mt* 18:21-35). We see this with the Apostles Peter and Paul who both failed Christ but who did not remain paralysed by their failings. Rather they were transformed by Christ's mercy and by his renewed faith in them after they had fallen (cf. *Jn* 21:15-17; *Ga* 1:11-24). This was the mercy and forgiveness that they proclaimed to all as part of their preaching (cf. *Ac* 2:38; 13:38).

With this forgiveness that we receive from God and extend to others, we are freed from anger, guilt, shame, bitterness and other emotionally destructive feelings such as hatred and revenge. Once the merciful love and power of Christ is invited into wounds of hurt then the cycle is broken of inflicting hurt on those who have inflicted it on us. This is what Jesus did by his Passion and death – he filtered out hatred, violence, injustice and cruelty by absorbing it into himself before giving back to the world the gifts of peace, blessing and forgiveness. This is the cycle of violence he broke and in doing so he changed the course of history. By that same power at work in his disciples today, we too can break the cycle by making sure we do not cause the same hurt to others as we ourselves have endured.

In order to do this, we need to learn Jesus' art of distinguishing between the sin and the sinner. With his Spirit we learn to forgive the wrong done to us without denying the wrong that was committed. This is a crucially important distinction to make. Many think that the invitation to forgive another who wronged them is beyond their ability because to do so would mean to minimise or deny the hurt that was caused to them. This is not what Christian forgiveness asks of us. We often hear the catchphrase "forgive and forget" – a pithy phrase which we think comes from the Gospel or the lips of Jesus. This is not true. Jesus asks us to forgive as we ourselves have been forgiven but he did not ask us to forget. What this means is that while we forgive with the help of God's grace, the process of healing is not about pretending that the hurt never happened. Rather it is about coming to the place where it no longer affects us.

Thankfully, there are many examples of heroic forgiveness in our recent history. In May 1981, Pope John Paul II was shot and seriously wounded in St Peter's Square in Rome by a man named Ali Agca. After his recovery, John Paul II visited Agca in prison and offered him forgiveness. In Northern Ireland during the Troubles, a committed Christian named Gordon Wilson publicly forgave those who killed his daughter Marie in a bomb attack in Enniskillen in

November 1987. In 1990 on his release from prison in South Africa, Nelson Mandela set on a course of reconciliation with all fellow citizens of his country in order to build peace and reconciliation which he continued later as president of South Africa. He likened the choice of harbouring resentment and revenge to remaining in a prison of his own making.[42]

These three people alone have inspired millions on their journey towards forgiveness and have witnessed to its power to heal society and transform lives. They chose not to seek revenge or to inflict on others what was inflicted on them. Although they never denied or minimised the injustices they suffered, they made a graced decision to become instruments of healing. By breaking the cycle of hurt, they became witnesses to hope, to the power of good over evil and the victory of love over hate.

Yet we know that while these examples of successful outcomes is where we aspire to arrive, the journey to get there is hard. Forgiveness of someone who has hurt us does not come easy and is one of the most challenging aspects of being a Christian. In the Gospels, Jesus asked us to forgive those who wrong us and left us the supreme example of doing

---

[42] N. Mandela, *Long Walk to Freedom*, McDonald Purnell, South Africa, 1994.

so himself. As he was being crucified, he cried out, "Father, forgive them for they know not what they do" (*Lk* 23:34). Jesus forgave his killers and after his resurrection he offered peace to those who had denied and failed him. How can we begin to forgive like this?

Again, Jesus shows us the way. He assures us that God is merciful and forgives us when we ask. Then he asks us to forgive others as we have been forgiven ourselves. This is challenging because the ability to extend forgiveness to others depends on our being in touch with our own sinfulness and shadow side. It requires us to know that we have no right to withhold the gift of mercy that we ourselves have received: "Should not you have had mercy on your fellow servant, as I had mercy on you?" (cf. *Mt* 18:33). This requires that we enter deeply within ourselves and humbly acknowledge our own brokenness, darkness and need for forgiveness. It means allowing the light of God's grace to touch our inner wounds.

For St Catherine of Siena, if we try too eagerly for spiritual perfection while "devoid of humility" and ignoring our imperfections, we will end up in "mental confusion and darkness". Why? Because we have attempted "to go upwards before going downwards".[43] For Catherine, this inner journey down into our

---

[43] *Letter* T343 to Raimond of Capua. Cited in P. Murray, *In the Grip of Light*, p. 29.

imperfections makes us more compassionate and so better disposed to forgive others: "Human weakness allows those who are in some way afflicted to acquire humility and self-knowledge…It makes them kind and not cruel towards their neighbours so that they are compassionate with them in their struggles".[44] For St Teresa of Avila (1515-1582), "it is absurd to think that we can enter heaven without first entering our own souls – without getting to know ourselves and reflecting upon the wretchedness of our nature… continually imploring his mercy".[45] For the saints therefore, being grounded in our own imperfections not only leads us to know God and his mercy but brings us into closer solidarity with the rest of humanity who struggle as we do.

Christianity is good news for those who have been hurt and who carry emotional scars. It gives us a way of dealing with negative baggage that leaves us free. Because of Jesus, we know that God is merciful and forgives us joyfully. He showed heroic forgiveness himself to those who killed him. He asks us to forgive others as we have been forgiven ourselves and "to

---

[44] *Dialogue of Divine Providence.* Cited in P. Murray, ed., *Scars*, Bloomsbury, London, 2014, pp. 43-44.

[45] Teresa of Avila, *Interior Castle*, 2, 1, 11 in D. Billy, ed., *Interior Castle: The Classic Text with Spiritual Commentary*, Ave Maria Press, Indiana, 2007, p. 68.

think of ourselves as an army of the forgiven".[46] Our faith shows us how to distinguish between the harm caused and the one who caused it. At all times, the healing Spirit of Christ, that restores and touches our knotted spirits, is offered to us. His infinite mercy is the antidote to every form of anger and hurt; it is balm for the scars that sear the soul.

---

[46] Pope Francis, *Rejoice and Be Glad*, 82.

6. Never Alone

A sixth resource that comes with faith is the support it provides through community. Much depression and many mental health problems are made worse by isolation and feeling we are suffering alone. To illustrate the point, it is known that there are higher rates of depression among those who are separated, divorced or alienated from friends and family.[47] In fact, the problem of loneliness has become so acute that governments are taking action. In January 2018, British Prime Minister Theresa May announced the appointment to her cabinet of a 'Minister of Loneliness' to tackle a sad reality of modern life, namely the isolation of so many people. This problem is not confined to Britain but is endemic in much of Western society.

Christians believe in a God of relationship – of Father, Son and Holy Spirit who share a life of communion and love. Faith and baptism draw us into that communion of love, uniting us to God and

---

[47] See A. Kheriaty, *The Catholic Guide to Depression*, p. 27.

to others who share that relationship with us. At the very beginning of the Bible, God's word tells us that "it is not good that man should be alone" (*Gn* 2:18). It is crystal clear: isolation is not good for us. Before the Fall, there was harmony and communion between Adam and Eve. After their sin, we see the first rupture in human relationships with alienation and mutual blame. But immediately after, God promised a redeemer who would heal this wound and restore communion that was damaged (cf. *Gn* 3:15).

We are creatures who thirst for this intimacy with God and others; we are made for relationships. The Psalmist prays, "O God, you are my God for you I long. For you my soul is thirsting like a dry weary land without water" (*Ps* 63:1). In the Gospels, Jesus recognises our loneliness and declares that this longing for intimacy will be uniquely satisfied by faith in him: "I am the bread of life. No one who comes to me will ever hunger" (*Jn* 5:35); "Let anyone who is thirsty come to me! Let anyone who believes in me come and drink!" (*Jn* 7:37-38). Here is the dynamism of the human spirit St Augustine described as being satisfied only by union with God: "You have made us for yourself O Lord and our hearts are restless until they rest in thee".[48] To be lonely therefore can be

[48] Augustine, *Confessions* 1, 1, 1 in J.K. Ryan, ed. and trans., *The Confessions of Saint Augustine*, p. 43.

understood positively as a built-in mechanism in our nature that draws us continually to intimacy with God.

As we are drawn deeper into intimacy with God, we also form relationships with each other in the Church. Because we are common children of our heavenly Father, we are all brothers and sisters in Christ (cf. *Ga* 3:27ff). This truth is first expressed in our families and in our local parish community understood as a "family of families".[49] Community is also experienced in the unity of the whole Christian family around the world. Within that community is a spirit that unites us in faith and fosters a sense of belonging to a people who cherish each other. We know them and they know us. This spirit of unity is not static but is preserved by fidelity to "the teaching of the Apostles, to the brotherhood, to the breaking of bread and to the prayers" (*Ac* 2:42). By our common faith, fraternity, by the celebration of the Eucharist and our common life of prayer, we become and remain one body, one spirit in Christ.

By extension, this communion is so strong that it connects us with the saints in every time and place who are our friends and join us in adoration of God. In the Church, each of us can say: "Surrounded, led and guided by the friends of God...I do not have to

---

[49] Pope Francis, *The Joy of Love*, 87.

carry alone what, in truth, I could never carry alone. All the saints of God are there to protect me, sustain me and to carry me".[50]

The glue that unites all Christians is the Holy Spirit of communion, the bond of love between the Father and the Son that is poured out on the Church. This gift of the Spirit enables us "to think of our brothers and sisters in faith within the profound unity of the Mystical Body and therefore as those who are part of me".[51] For all Christian Churches, a sense of welcome and belonging is fundamentally important along with the provision of times and spaces where people can meet, befriend each other and provide mutual support and encouragement. Here is the essence of parish and community life as a network of supportive relationships. Just as disturbance of relationship is a central feature of many mental health problems, so friendship, support and community are important contributors to a positive and healthy mind. Church communities can be and indeed are places where people with mental health problems feel accepted and supported in the same way the community supports people with any other illness. Pope Francis calls the Church to be "A Mother with an open heart... who

---

[50] Pope Benedict XVI, *Homily at Mass for the Solemn Inauguration of the Petrine Ministry*, 24th April 2005. See also *Heb* 12:1.

[51] Pope John Paul II, *Novo Millennio Ineunte*, 43.

must accompany with attention and care the weakest of her children who show signs of a wounded and troubled love…those who have lost their way or who are in the midst of a storm".[52] On this path of life together we walk side by side "with our brothers and sisters who reach out for someone to take their hand and become a companion on the way".[53] Yet there is still much to be done by faith communities to walk this journey with those who suffer from mental illness and to remove the stigma that prevents it from being considered worthy of the same prayer and care directed to people who have physical illnesses.

Being incorporated in the Church today models an alternative to our culture of individualism where the self is at the centre. When the relational dimensions of humanity get forgotten in this culture, we slowly cut off our own oxygen supply in ways that stifle the spirit and suffocate the soul. We become turned in on ourselves and become lonely which causes us emotional pain. Our culture may prize independence as one of the greatest goods but the Gospel treasures the gift of interdependence that keeps us united. In the Church, we learn how to be intimate with the Lord through prayer and to realise the truth of the paradox pithily

---

[52] Pope Francis, *The Joy of the Gospel*, 46-49; *The Joy of Love*, 291.

[53] Pope Francis, *Misericordia et Misera*, 16.

described by St Ambrose: "I am never less alone than when I seem to be alone".[54] This is why Pope Francis, in the opening paragraph of *The Joy of the Gospel* says about Christ, "Those who accept his offer of salvation are set free from sin, sorrow, inner emptiness and loneliness".[55] In our Church communities we celebrate friendship with him and learn to share in ways that counter the problem of loneliness and isolation. In the family of the Church there is the opportunity to make new friends, find our future wives and husbands and to become a contrasting society that offers an antidote to the loneliness so prevalent in our society.

The Gospel is good news for those who suffer from loneliness for it offers the gift of community and support that we need. It is a sign of hope for a Western world that is beginning to acknowledge the problems arising from a culture of individualism and where loneliness is becoming the pathology of our age. May people who feel isolated and need the support of others find that support and understanding in every faith community. May people who suffer from any form of mental illness experience welcome, care and compassion. Together may we model through the

---

[54] Ambrose, *Letter* 49. Cited in *Directory for the Ministry and Life of Priests*, Libreria Editrice Vaticana, Vatican City, 2014, p. 75.

[55] Pope Francis, *The Joy of the Gospel*, 1.

Church an existence where we belong to each other, care for each other but ultimately belong together to Christ who satisfies our hungers and promised that he would never abandon us.

7. The Joy of Virtue and Misery of Vice

A seventh dimension of mental health that faith illuminates is the link between leading a virtuous life and the experience of happiness. This link is emphasised by Christians because of who we understand ourselves to be. As human beings, our actions, behaviours and habits impact on our general wellbeing for good or for ill. Therefore our health, including our mental health, is affected by our lifestyles and choices. Our actions affect our health because our actions are in accordance with our true nature or they are not. When our actions are harmonious with our human nature then contentment and happiness flows; when our actions are contrary to our nature then misery ensues.

A general example of this principle would be the importance of leading a balanced life. If I drink too much, smoke and take little exercise then my physical health will suffer. And if my physical health declines then this will also have a negative effect on my mental health. That is why people in the caring professions help patients reclaim a more balanced and healthy lifestyle where care of the body, mind and soul are always kept in view. For Catholics, this incarnational principle is foundational; ours is not a religion of the spirit only. We take very seriously our embodied existence and the relational dimension of our lives. We are not machines or units of autonomy but understand our whole existence in relationship to God, ourselves, others and the created world we are part of. In the words of Pope Francis, "everything is interconnected".[56]

A specific dimension of our general wellbeing is our mental health and how our moral lives and choices impact on it. There is much evidence that this link between morality and mental health is neglected or at least downplayed in public debate on the issue today. Talking about vice and sin is unpopular because we think it pronounces judgement and is intolerant. "Who are you to tell me how to live!"; "Who are you to tell me how to be happy?" In our culture that prizes individual freedom, we argue that people should be free to make their own choices to be happy as they see fit. The problem with this argument is that it ignores the human nature that we all have in common. It tends to see our freedom as an end in itself and

---

[56] Pope Francis, *Laudato Si*, 70.

divorced from the human nature it is part of. This was not always the case.

Before Christianity, Plato (c. 428-347 BC) argued that human behaviour is related to human contentment by pointing out that justice always makes us happy.[57] For St Augustine, happiness is more than a feeling but is always linked to the truth: "Joy in the truth is the happy life. This is joy in you, who are the truth, O God my light".[58] For St Thomas Aquinas (1225-1274), all the prescriptions and prohibitions of the Gospel are ordered to our joy or what he calls *beatitudo* – blessedness. According to Thomas, the moral life is about the way we should live in order to attain the happiness that God wants us to enjoy. Thomas clarified that this joy comes about through being faithful to our human nature made in the image and likeness of God and designed for blessed communion with God in this life and the next. He is at pains to explain how wealth, honour, fame, power, pleasure or even moral virtue alone cannot make us happy. Nothing or no one but God can fulfil our thirst for joy and complete contentment.[59] Here is the invitation to order our

---

[57] Plato, *The Republic*, Book 2, 358a in A. Bloom (trans.), *The Republic of Plato*, Basic Books, New York, 1991, p. 36.

[58] *Confessions*, 10, 23, 33, in J.K. Ryan, ed. and trans., *The Confessions of Saint Augustine*, p. 252.

[59] *Summa Theologiae*, I-II, 2, 1-8.

lives along the domains of the commandments and beatitudes of justice, truth, peace, mercy and love as the gateway to authentic happiness.

On this roadmap, we attain happiness by living in accordance with virtues and habits that bring us into right relationship with God and others. Practising the virtues forges character and facilitates the practice of the good. The Catholic tradition has outlined three of these virtues as attaining to proper union with God, the source of our joy. These are the theological virtues of faith, hope and charity. The other four are known as the cardinal virtues – prudence, justice, fortitude and temperance.[60] These are the building blocks of moral choices that safeguard our happiness and peace.

In the modern era, the focus has shifted from the classical approach of how certain virtues and actions make us happy to the freedom to pursue the happiness as each individual sees it. And so the pursuit of absolute freedom by the individual becomes so dominant that we forget the true nature of happiness that freedom is meant to serve. Very often in the name of expanding liberty and desire to master and control our fates, the choices we make in the name of freedom have become cages of our captivity. Here is the paradox that many discover – that in our quest to be free, some of the

---

[60] Cf. *CCC*, 1805-1809; 1812-1829.

choices we make and habits we develop entangle us in slavery. We need only think of the many addictions that we are vulnerable to in our culture today. While liberal lifestyles without discipline and commitment might initially seem attractive, so many of us painfully discover the truth that bad habits and addictions drag us down and pathetically fail to deliver the joy they promise.

The Christian Tradition also insists that our conscience is a mechanism that teaches us what are the right choices to make and what choices or habits to avoid. The conscience can anticipate which actions will bring sadness and which will bring joy. For St Ignatius of Loyola (1491-1556), when we make bad choices we must welcome the prick of conscience and note the misery that sin produces. This desolation is purifying.[61] In this light, not all guilt is negative. It is like pain to the body, telling us something is wrong. As Pope Pius XII taught, "Guilt is the consciousness of having violated a higher law, by which, nevertheless, one recognises himself as being bound, a consciousness which can find expression in suffering and psychic disorder".[62]

---

[61] 'Spiritual Exercises: First Week' in P. Wolff, ed., *The Spiritual Exercises of Saint Ignatius*, Liguori Publications, Missouri, 1997, pp. 18-28.

[62] Pope Pius XII, *Address to the Fifth International Congress on Psychotherapy and Clinical Psychology*, 13th April 1953.

In the spiritual order, honesty forces us to acknowledge the reality of sin which is the deadliest sort of pathology since it attacks the soul and drains its joy.[63] In the professional opinion of one Catholic psychiatrist, "Much mental distress or disorder, including some cases of depression, are caused or sustained by a person trying to live a series of contradictions".[64] By living these contradictions, the soul is divided from the spirit and body in a way that brings stress, guilt, shame and depression. So while the confessional was never meant to be a cure for neuroses or mental health problems, it can be argued that the psychiatrist's couch was never meant to absolve sin; but absolution is what people need as much as clinical treatment if their mental problems are being caused by moral conflicts. As Pope Pius XII wisely advised, there comes a time when "the doctor should direct his patient towards God and to those who have the power to remit the fault itself in the name of God".[65]

---

[63] The *Catechism of the Catholic Church* describes envy, one of the traditional seven deadly sins, as a sadness. *CCC*, 2540. St Thomas Aquinas wrote that "sin cuts deep because it harms our very self, not just our feelings". *STh* I-I, 39, 3.

[64] A. Kheriaty, *The Catholic Guide to Depression*, p. 172.

[65] Pope Pius XII, *Address to the Fifth International Congress on Psychotherapy and Clinical Psychology*, 13th April 1953.

The Gospel is good news because it points us to the good life of genuine happiness. It also shows us the way to live it and what to avoid. The teachings of Christianity guide us to develop behaviours and habits that safeguard our joy and urge us to avoid vices that bring misery and sadness. For the sake of God's joy we have been made to "have life and have it to the full" (*Jn* 10:10).

8. Getting Our House in Order

The eighth resource provided by Christian faith is the emphasis on right order. We have all heard of the catchphrase "get your house in order first". It describes the urgent need to sort ourselves out by identifying what elements in our lives we need to change or prioritise before we can help others. The phrase also points to a more literal truth of the importance of order as a prerequisite to a clear mind and a sound mental health. A simple example is tidying my room or my desk in the office. The more I put some order or shape in it, the better I feel I can focus on my work and plan my day; or putting order in my day with the help of my diary. It helps me to organise commitments but also helps me retain control of when I exercise, rest, read, call friends and pray. From this everyday experience, I know the truth that tranquillity and harmony do flow from right order.

This concept of right order is not new. As early as the fourth century, St Augustine wrote that peace comes from *tranquillitas ordinis*….the tranquillity of order. He writes, "Peace between man and God is the well-ordered obedience of faith to eternal law…The peace of the celestial city is the perfectly ordered and harmonious enjoyment of God, and of one another in God. The peace of all things is the tranquillity of order".[66] For Augustine, not all things in our lives are equally important. Neither are all relationships in our lives on the same level of priority.

Similarly, St Thomas Aquinas developed this idea by referring to the *ordinis caritas* or the order of charity – that we love things in their proper order if happiness is to be ours.[67] First is the love and worship of God, for "He is loved as the cause of happiness". This confirms the teaching of Scripture in both the Old Testament and the teaching of Jesus who restated that the first and most important commandment was to "love God with all your heart, with all your soul and with all your mind" (*Mt* 22:37; *Lk* 10:27). This was the first of the commandments – not by being first on a list but by being the commandment that gives right order to all the rest. For Thomas, God is loved first and most whereas "our neighbour is loved as receiving together with us a share of happiness from God".[68] After love of

[66] Augustine, *The City of God*, 19, 14, Book on Demand, Paris, 2018, p. 560.

[67] T. Aquinas, *STh* II-II, 26.

[68] *STh*. II-II, 26, 2.

God there is the love of the self, one's spouse, children, parents, family, friends, and strangers. For Thomas, this natural order of loves that is so important in creation will be preserved, transformed and perfected in heaven.[69] Therefore, preparing for heaven and experiencing its delights in this life involves loving – not all things equally, but all things and people in their right order.

In an increasingly egalitarian culture that regards any form of hierarchy with suspicion, this call to a certain order is a hard sell. And yet we understand the language of loving our families first and who comes first in our lives, namely those we love most. We instinctively know that not everything and everyone in our lives exists on the same level. In this framework, hierarchy is natural and necessary, and knowing this to be true does not contradict that other truth we adhere to, which is that all people are equal.

The practical consequence of this call to right order is that it challenges us to consider how we spend our time and our money. What we spend most of our money on or most of our time doing is a good indicator of what we love most. If St Thomas is right and if our first love is God then we might ask ourselves how much time we dedicate to prayer? Have I forgotten

---

[69] *STh*. II-II, 26, 13.

to prioritise my relationship with the Lord? Do other people come first or have I tried to supplant his love with love for the things he has made? If our families and those we love matter to us, how much time do we spend with them?

This call to right order necessarily has an organisational element to it. Feeling better, having greater peace and stronger mental health means putting the simple things in place and in their right order. This can mean developing the habit of daily prayer and meditation, keeping our desk and homes tidy, not doing too much of anything or allowing some commitment to consume all our time. It could mean going to bed early and getting enough sleep, having regular meals and a healthy diet. It could mean going for a walk, taking physical exercise every day or taking up a hobby. It could mean fasting from screen time with our smartphones and electronic devices. Restoring right order means taking the time to nurture our relationships with family and friends. All of these components are key to our mental health, emotional well-being and enjoying a balanced life that is healthy in body, mind and soul.

Finally, there is evidence that the more our lives are rightly ordered, the firmer are the boundaries of the self, with a stronger locus of self-control.[70] Research reveals a significant and positive relationship between religious belief and this internal locus of control.[71] Religious faith instils moral values and increases self-discipline.[72] Christianity calls us to be free and responsible. It provides a foundation of love for a person's life and offers a guide of how to live that love by our attitudes, words and choices. Love of God and neighbour provides a moral compass that directs our actions towards charity and service.

Experience also shows that this proper order in our lives can easily be disrupted, with a subsequent weakening of our locus of self-control. A lack of discipline and bad habits make us more vulnerable to actions that are not consistent with our true selves and

---

[70] Thomas Merton (1915-1968) wrote extensively about the important concept of finding the centre or the inner locus of who we are before God. "In this most inward 'I', my own solitude meets the solitude of every other man and the solitude of God. Hence it is beyond division, limitation and selfish affirmation". T. Merton, *Disputed Questions*, Farrar, Straus and Cudahy, New York, 1960, p. 207.

[71] See L.E. Jackson – R.D. Coursey, 'The relationship of God control and internal locus of control to intrinsic religious motivation, coping and purpose in life' in *Journal for the Scientific Study of Religion*, 27, (1998), pp. 399-410.

[72] "Religious participation...instils moral values, increases coping skills and decreases the likelihood of turning to alcohol or other drugs during times of stress". H.G. Koenig – M.E. McCullough – D.B. Larson, *Handbook of Religion and Health*, Oxford, Oxford University Press, 2001, p.180.

sometimes contradict our deepest held values. Catholic anthropology describes the emotions and appetites that rebel against the intellect and will as "disordered passions"; they tend to make human thinking, willing and feeling become fragmented. As St Paul describes the dilemma, "The good thing I want to do, I never do; the evil thing I do not want, that is what I do" (*Rm* 7:19). Here is the divided will in us that spills over into fragmented and disordered relationships. If temperance is not part of our lives then disordered passions can compromise our freedom, leading to destructive addictions and compulsions which cause misery.

For Christians, the Gospel is good news because the commandments and the Beatitudes are not mere laws but blueprints for the happiness God wishes us to enjoy. They are antidotes to chaos and slavery, and key to a well-ordered life which leads to blessedness and peace. That is why the Psalmist could write, "Had your law not been my delight, I would have perished in my misery" (*Ps* 119:92).

9. Prayer and Liturgy
as Rites of Passage

A ninth resource that comes from Christian faith is the practice of prayer and the celebration of rituals and rites of passage. Viewing the experience of life as a pilgrimage, along that journey there are key moments that have a human need to be marked and celebrated. This need is acknowledged not just by Christianity but also by other faith traditions such as Judaism and Islam and indeed by many cultures whether they include a faith dimension or not.[73]

Concerning how we see the value of ritual, one of the great challenges the Church faces is how to connect people more meaningfully with its life of ritual and sacraments. Many people, especially the young, no longer participate meaningfully or regularly in the rites the Church has to offer.

Yet there is a dawning realisation that the absence of significant moments of ceremony in life leaves us

---

[73] The anthropological roots of rites of passage have been studied by Victor Turner in *The Ritual Process: Structure and Anti-Structure*, Routledge & Kegan Paul, London, 1969.

disconnected, confused, alone and adrift. Without moments of pause and prayer that mark the passage of time, everything collapses into a dull sameness, when Sunday is the same as Monday. This dull sameness leaves the human spirit at sea with no points of reference that differentiate the passage of time and the significant moments in life. In the face of this deadening effect caused by an absence of rituals, there is increasing appreciation of rituals that mark the changes of life and the movement from one transition to another. These are milestones on the journey that acknowledge and name what is past and look forward to the future. Such rituals lead to a revitalisation of the spirit that comes with a certain closure on the past and the anticipation of the future with hope.

The prayer and sacramental life of the Church is rich in marking the passage of time and the rhythms of life. These sacramental moments are open to God's grace, his action through the power of his Spirit. They are moments integrated into the whole mystery of life that is permeated by the presence of God and his saving work in the universe. They are moments therefore of prayer and worship. As the *Catechism of the Catholic Church* explains,

> "The liturgical celebration involves signs and symbols relating to creation (candles, water, fire),

human life (washing, anointing, breaking bread) and the history of salvation (the rites of the Passover). Integrated into the world of faith and taken up by the power of the Holy Spirit, these cosmic elements, human rituals, and gestures of remembrance of God become bearers of the saving and sanctifying action of Christ".[74]

This means that the rites of the Church are connected to the whole journey of life from beginning to end. For example, the celebration of new life is marked by baptism; the Eucharist marks the end of one week with the beginning of another; moving into adulthood is marked by Confirmation; moments of commitment marked by marriage and holy orders; times of sickness, pain and injury marked by anointing and forgiveness; finally, the funeral rites of the Church mark the ultimate transition from this life to the next. In all of these sacramental celebrations, the symbols and signs of the rites point to and connect us with spiritual realities that are present and active. These can be moments that are therapeutic, healing and joyful, that build community and have a positive effect on our mental health and well-being. These are milestones on our journey that afford us time to reflect on what has been and look forward to what lies ahead. Above all,

[74] *CCC*, 1189.

they are moments when we intentionally connect with the source of all life who is God Himself.

Despite the fall-off in people engaging with the ritual life of the Church, hope comes from the many people who still present their children for baptism, first communion, confirmation, anointing, healing and the rites of passage surrounding death. There are also signs of hope that the majority are still open to sacramental moments like the blessing of homes, farms, cars, engagement rings, etc. The challenge for Christianity is to initiate people into a habit of ritual that marks not just the key moments of life but also the key moments of every day from the moment we wake up in the morning to when we go to bed at night. That is why the Church speaks of the sanctification of time and how it is marked by prayer "so that the whole course of the day and night is made holy by the praise of God".[75]

There is evidence that those who participate in rites, rituals and prayers have better mental health than those who don't. One research study found that, out of 3,000 women who regularly attended Church, mortality was more than a third lower than the general population.[76] Research also found that the risk of suicide in people

---

[75] *Sacrosanctum concilium*, 84.

[76] See W.J. Strawbridge-R.D. Cohen-S.J. Shema-G.A. Kaplan, 'Frequent attendance at religious services and mortality over 28 years' in *American Journal of Public Health*, 87, pp. 957-961.

suffering from depression is lowered by participation in rites of prayer, worship and religious faith.[77] The most recent findings from Harvard University also confirm that frequent attendance at religious services is associated with lower subsequent risk of deaths from despair.[78]

There are many reasons why this is true, one of them being the opportunity to express gratitude. When we pray we give expression to gratitude which counteracts self-pity, narcissistic tendencies and pride. The central ritual in our Catholic tradition is the Eucharist, which is a prayer of thanksgiving. Prayer is also an opportunity to express our feelings honestly before God. For this the Psalms are extremely helpful as they offer a vocabulary and grammar to give voice to emotional sorrow: "My heart pounds within me; death's terrors fall upon me. Fear and trembling overwhelm me; shuddering sweeps over me" (*Ps* 55); "Out of the depths I cry to you O Lord; O Lord hear my voice!" (*Ps* 130:1) Conversely Scripture can provide

---

[77] See A. Kheriaty, *The Catholic Guide to Depression*, pp. 89-99.

[78] The results of this study were published in May 2020. Of 66,492 female registered nurses and 43,141 male health care professionals in the US, attendance at religious services at least once per week was associated with a 68% lower hazard of death from despair among women and a 33% lower hazard among men compared with those who never attend. See *https://jamanetwork.com/journals/jamapsychiatry/fullarticle/2765488*

us with the language of uplifting gratitude and praise: "I thank you Lord with all my heart; I sing praise to you" (*Ps* 34:1-3); "Come, let us sing for joy to the Lord; let us shout aloud to the rock of our salvation. Let us come before him with thanksgiving and extol him with music and song" (*Ps* 95:1-2). Having grappled with darkness, in God's Word we discover hope – "For I know the plans I have for you, says the Lord, plans for peace and not disaster, to give you a future and a hope" (*Jr* 29:11). For the one who trusts in God, sorrow and pain will finally be overcome (cf. *Is* 35:10; 51:11). We may grieve now but sooner or later "your sorrow will turn to joy" (*Jn* 16:20).

These are the prayers and sacred texts, distilled over centuries of experience, that timelessly reflect the vagaries of the human condition. That is why in the fourth century St Athanasius said that "the psalms seem to me to be like a mirror, in which the person using them can see himself and the stirrings of his own heart; he can recite them against the background of his own emotions".[79]

To conclude this chapter, the book of Ecclesiastes states that "there is a season for everything, a time for giving birth, a time for dying" and a time for

---

[79] St Athanasius, *Letter to Marcellinus*, 11. Cited by Pope Pius X in *Divino Afflatu*, 1st November 1911, *Acta Apostolicie Sedis*, Vatican, vol. 3, pp. 633-37.

everything in between (cf. *Qo* 3:1-8); the Church's life of ritual and sacraments gives expression to those times of birth, death and other milestones. These are the moments when God blesses us and transforms us by his grace that flows through the events of life. They are moments when the human spirit is supported as it travels along her pilgrim journey. They are gifts from God to his Church to help us stay on the right path and point us in the right direction.

10. The Hope that Saves

Finally, Christian faith is a wellspring of hope without which the human spirit disintegrates. "In hope we are saved" St Paul wrote to the Romans and so it remains today (*Rm* 8:24). For the Christian who suffers, trials are not ends in themselves but temporary moments of transformation to be embraced as the means to make us more perfect in love and more perfectly united to the source of love who is God. This is the source of our hope – that all suffering takes place with the future in view where God's kingdom will be realised, where suffering will come to an end and give way to the joy of perfect union with the God of love and beauty.

For the believer, hope is grounded in the conviction that the ultimate victory belongs to Christ, a victory he has already won on the cross. It is a hope founded on the promise of Jesus at the Last Supper: "In the world you will have tribulation, but take courage for I have overcome the world" (*Jn* 16:33). One Catholic Christian who was a witness to this hope was St John

Paul II: he lived through the loss of all his family, the horror of the Second World War, Communism, being shot and almost killed, bowel cancer, Parkinson's disease and many more trials, yet he never lost hope. To thousands of young people gathered for World Youth Day in Toronto in 2002 he said,

> "Although I have lived through much darkness under harsh totalitarian regimes, I have seen enough evidence to be unshakably convinced that no difficulty, no fear is so great that it can completely suffocate the hope that springs eternal in the hearts of the young…do not let that hope die! Stake your lives on it!"[80]

Here is the hope of the resurrection that extends back to the first Christians including the disciples who met Christ on the road to Emmaus (cf. *Lk* 24:13ff). When Jesus met them and walked with them, their faces were downcast and sad for their hopes and expectations of Jesus had been shattered with his death. But after they recognised him at the breaking of bread, their hopes were re-born. They turned back to Jerusalem, re-joined the Church community and began to preach the new hope they had discovered. This was the hope of the early saints, the martyrs, the missionaries and

---

[80] Pope John Paul II, *Homily at Closing Mass of World Youth Day*, Downsview Park, Toronto, Canada, Sunday 28th July 2002.

prophets of the Church. It is the same hope that brings us forward today and gives us the courage to face every trial.

Many believers who suffer from mental illness testify that had it not been for the hope that comes from their Christian faith, they may not have survived. Countless people of faith have seen in their suffering the seeds of a future of hope – that the sorrow they experience will give way eventually to joy (cf. *Jn* 16:20). This is not a form of wishful thinking that consoles us in present misery but a real act of faith that sees mental suffering as a participation in Christ's anguish that precedes a form of new life in the future. For the Christian, the Gospel gives us hope and gives life a trajectory towards that definitive future. In the words of Pope Benedict XVI, "The present, even if it is arduous, can be lived and accepted if it leads towards a goal". For this reason "the one who has hope lives differently".[81] Unlike most root causes of physical illnesses, there is no prescription or medical cure for a lack of hope. The only cure for a lack of hope is hope itself – the theological virtue of hope which can be infused only by God's grace that comes with faith.

There are signs that our Western world is struggling to find hope, while in the throes of a pandemic of

---

[81] Pope Benedict XVI, *Spe salvi*, 1.

despair. Symptoms of this despair include suicide, euthanasia, drug abuse and widespread depression. Evidence for this comes from the studies of a psychiatrist who carried out a long term study of 800 suicidal patients to determine which risk factors were most closely linked to suicide. The most dangerous factor he identified was their sense of hopelessness.[82]

For the believer, hope born of faith in God is a hope that sees beyond present difficulties however bad they might be. "Faith in Jesus leads to a greater hope, to a certainty based not on our own qualities and skills but on the Word of God, on the invitation that comes from him".[83] Witnesses to Easter hope already anticipate the new future that will emerge from the power of faith in the risen Lord. For this reason, hope is the "sure and steadfast anchor of the soul...that enters...where Jesus has gone as a forerunner on our behalf" (*Heb* 6:19-20). And so, while we rejoice in hope, we must be patient in tribulation (cf. *Rm* 12:12), sure in the knowledge that God who raised Jesus from the dead will give us a share of his victory of light over darkness.

"Let us not allow ourselves to be robbed of hope!"[84] Christianity gives us reason to hope because

---

[82] See A. Kheriaty, *The Catholic Guide to Depression*, p. 99.

[83] Pope Francis, *Christ is Alive*, 141.

[84] Pope Francis, *The Joy of the Gospel*, 86.

of Christ's triumph over suffering and death that he promised he would share with us. When the shadow of the cross falls on our minds and lives it is only because there is a light on the other side of that cross. The shadow will come and go, but the light of the resurrection will shine forever. I end this chapter with inspiring words of hope from Pope Francis that he addresses to all of us:

"Christ is in you, he is with you and he never abandons you. However far you may wander, he is always there, the Risen One. He calls you and he waits for you to return to him and start over again. When you feel you are growing old out of sorrow, resentment or fear, doubt or failure, he will always be there to restore your strength and your hope".[85]

---

[85] Pope Francis, *Christ is alive*, 2.

Conclusion

According to psychiatrist Andrew Sims, "the advantageous effect of religious belief and spirituality on mental and physical health is one of the best kept secrets in psychiatry and medicine generally".[86]

This booklet has sought to tease out ten advantageous effects of Christian faith for mental health – God's unconditional love that is available to all; that God's love confers on us a basic identity that reveals who we are; that faith is a source of meaning; that every human experience including mental anguish has been assumed and redeemed by God in Christ; with faith in Christ comes the gift of forgiveness and the power to forgive; believing draws into a supportive faith community where we are not alone; that faith highlights the link between living a virtuous life and enjoying a happy mind; that faith moves us towards the right order necessary for peace and tranquillity; with Christian faith comes a life of

---

[86] A. Sims, *Is Faith a Delusion?*, p. 221.

prayer and ritual, essential for mental health and well-being; that Christian faith brings hope that lifts the spirit towards new horizons.

My hope is that this booklet will contribute to a growing awareness in the Church of the benefits of faith to mental health and a renewed confidence in contributing confidently to this important debate.